How the Old Man Learned to Smile

All rights reserved. No part of the book may be reproduced, stored in a retrieval system, or transmitted in any form or by any means, photocopying, photography, mechanical, recording, electronic, scanning, except in the case of brief quotations for the purpose of reviews or critical analysis or as permitted by the United States Copyright Act of 1976 and all other applicable international, federal, state and local laws, or with prior written permission from the publisher and author.

ISBN-13: 978-0-9823570-4-0

ISBN-10: 0982357044

Genre: Children's Books

Age Group: 3 to 7 (emotional intelligence and empathy building)

First Edition: April 2013

Printed in the United States of America

Copyright © 2013 Uwe Blesching, Ph.D.
Published by Logos Publishing House
Berkeley, California.

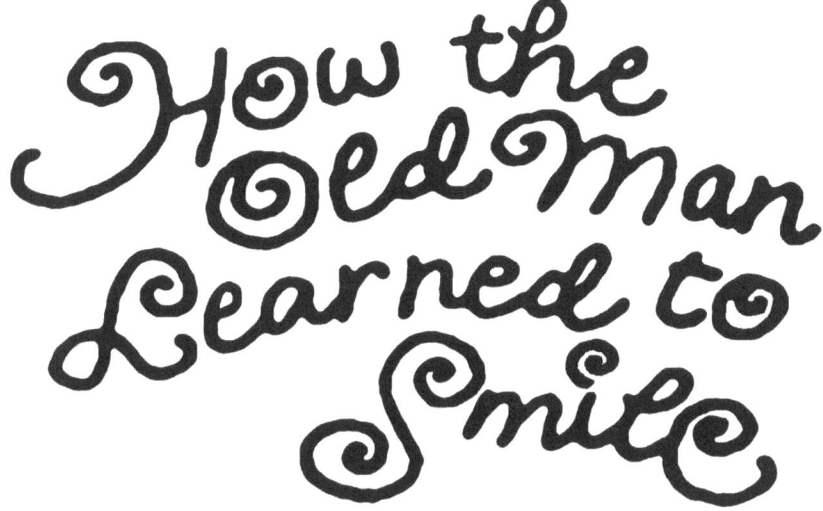

Written by Uwe Blesching
Illustrated by Kanna Aoki

Once upon a time, in the great valley between Purple Mountain and Lake Magia there was a village where there lived many cheerful people and one very grouchy old man.

The old man's face was sour with frowns. He never smiled and was friends with no one. Behind his house there was a beautiful tree with big branches full of gold and green leaves, which made magical whooshing sounds when the winds of the valley blew.

The old man did not let anyone near his tree, so when the children of the valley came to play under the great tree he was angry and ran after them with his broom yelling and shouting.

The scared children ran and ran to get away from the grouchy old man.

In time, the children no longer played under the great tree, they just laughed and played at the pond.

But there was one rather shy girl, who was new to the valley. This was Rose and her best friend Timber the cat. Rose was from a deeply wooded land where she loved to spend her days hearing the songs of the blowing wind in the leaves of the trees. To Rose, the great tree behind the old man's house was the only tree in the valley that felt like home.

Rose wondered about the old man, "Why didn't he want anyone to enjoy the great tree?"

So one day she snuck up to the tree and said: "perhaps YOU could do something so the old man will let us play here, and not frighten or scare us away anymore."

There was no wind, but she heard a faint flutter among the tree's leaves.

At that moment the old man came out of the house, broom in hand, and just as he opened his mouth to yell —

suddenly something happened to him..."

Tree magic was afoot. As the old man woke, he heard a little voice laughing. A small boy was jumping and playing, with a big smile on his face that reached from ear to ear!

He was having the time of his life! Behind the boy was a small tree. It looked like HIS tree when it was much smaller, with tiny branches and tender leaves.

"What a happy place," he said to himself. But then, like loud thunder, a grim voice boomed, "I told you a thousand times to be quiet!"

The little boy suddenly became quiet and sad, and this greatly upset the old man. He got up, took the little boy in his arms and hugged him, and said, "I'll make sure you will never need to be afraid to have a fun time again!"

The old man walked into the house of the booming voice, and, by goodness, it was his own father who was yelling, and the little boy was the old man himself when he was young. The old man went to his father and said, "You must be very careful to let your son play and be free, or he will become an angry, grouchy, and lonely man." The father could tell that the old man knew what he was talking about and of course, not wanting his son to grow up to be grouchy or lonely, he let his son play freely, since he loved him very much.

As the old man opened his eyes under the green and leafy sky, the children of the valley were looking at him closely, wondering what happened.

Then like the wind they ran away again, down the hill. The old man sat up and cried, "Wait, don't run away!" but they were too far away to hear him.

He began to cry and then noticing a cat beside him, he looked up. Rose was standing there. "Little girl, why didn't you run away like the others?" he asked.

"Because of tree magic, I'm not afraid of you anymore," she said with a smile. And with tears and laughter, the old man, Rose, and Timber the cat shared a great big hug. Their laughter sang louder and louder, down into the valley below and the children began to wonder.

Slowly, one by one, the children came back up the hill and found that the place they had learned to be afraid of had become a place of great happiness.

Then they played under the great tree, around the great tree, and even IN the great tree, playing and singing, as they always wanted.

Rose and Timber made many new friends but the old man and the tree were still their favorite.

The old man, who had a great big smile on his face that reached from ear to ear, said to himself, "Yes, it's never too late to have a happy childhood."